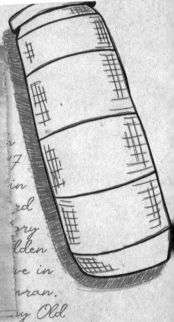

Jesus Was Born (Isaiah 7:14; Micah 5:2; Matthew 1:18–2:6)

Hundreds of years before Jesus was born, God told prophets to write about His plan to send His Son to be our Savior. Many years later an angel of the Lord appeared to Joseph. The angel told him Mary would have God's Son, and they were to name Him Jesus. Just as God promised Jesus was born in Bethlehem. God promised He would send His Son, and He did.

...y Old Testament scrolls were contained in the jars.

Bonus Verse
Isaiah 9:6a

Today's Point
Jesus is the Savior God promised.

1

UNEARTHING GOD'S PROMISES

Match the correct Bible verse to the prophecy.

Genesis 3:15

Genesis 12:3

Isaiah 9:7

Isaiah 35:5-6

Micah 5:2

Isaiah 61:8

Jesus would perform miracles.

Jesus would be born in Bethlehem.

Jesus would be the permanent covenant with God's people.

Jesus would crush the serpent.

Jesus would fulfill the promised worldwide blessing given to Abraham.

Jesus would come from the line of King David.

DIG SITE

FACTS ABOUT BETHLEHEM

1. Bethlehem means "House of Bread" in Hebrew.

2. Bethlehem had different names in the Old Testament: Ephrath (Genesis 35:16,19; 48:7), Bethlehem Ephrathah (Micah 5:2; Ruth 4:11), Bethlehem of Judah (1 Samuel 17:12), and "the city of David" (Luke 2:4).

3. The Book of Ruth primarily takes place in Bethlehem. Ruth was in the lineage of Jesus and was the great-grandmother to King David.

4. King David was born in Bethlehem. Samuel went to Bethlehem to anoint David as king.

5. The Church of The Nativity, which still stands, was constructed in Bethlehem by the Emperor Constantine and his mother is presumed to mark the birthplace of Jesus.

Jesus Healed a Blind Man (Psalm 146:8; Isaiah 35:5-6a; John 9:1-41)

Prophets wrote about what would happen when God's Son came to earth. They wrote about miracles He would perform such as healing people. When Jesus began His ministry, He did everything God said He would do. One day while in Jerusalem, Jesus passed a man who had been blind since birth. Jesus spat on the ground and made some mud. He spread the mud over the man's eyes and told the man to go wash in the Pool of Siloam. The man did as he was told, and he could see! The man told people what Jesus had done. Later, when the man saw Jesus, he worshiped Him.

If this man were not from God, he wouldn't be able to do
John 9:33

31.7710° N, 85.2347° E
Pool of Siloam

Bonus Verse
John 9:33

Today's Point
Jesus has the power God promised.

TRUE OR FALSE?

1. The pool was uncovered in 2004 when construction began to repair a damaged building.

2. The pool measures 500 feet long.

3. The pool was possibly used during Jesus' time as a site of ritual bathing.

4. The pool is fed by the Euphrates River through Hezekiah's tunnel.

5. The area around the pool contained ancient artifacts such as biblical-era coins with ancient Jewish writing, pottery shards, and a stone bottle cork, which helped to confirm the pool's identity.

RECORD KEEPING: THE POWER OF JESUS

Match the Bible verse to the correct event.

Turns water into wine	Widow's son raised to life	Healed a paralytic
Caused a fig tree to wither	Healed a man with withered hand	A girl is raised to life
Fed five thousand	Walked on the sea	Healed a servant's ear

Bible Verses

Mark 6:45-52
John 2:1-11
Matthew 9:2-8

Luke 7:11-17
Luke 22:50-51
John 6:5-14

Mark 3:1-6
Matthew 9:18-26
Matthew 21:18-22

Jesus Experienced Betrayal and Rejection
(Psalm 41:9; Isaiah 53:3,7; John 13; 18:1–19:16)

Jesus shared one last special supper with His disciples. During the meal Jesus explained that one of the disciples would betray Him. Jesus knew His betrayal and death would fulfill God's plan. After the meal, Jesus and all the disciples except for Judas went to the garden in Gethsemane. While they were there, Judas brought the soldiers to arrest Jesus and take Him to the high priest to begin the trials the prophets had written about many years before. Pilate, the Roman governor, tried to find a way to release Jesus, but the crowd shouted, "Crucify Him!" Jesus remained silent just as the prophecy said He would. Finally, Pilate gave in to the people's demands, and Jesus was handed over to the soldiers to be crucified.

Bonus Verse
Matthew 20:28

Today's Point
Jesus knew what would happen and still followed God's plan.

ARTIFACTS OF SERVICE

Look up each verse and record what each says about serving others.

Philippians 2:4

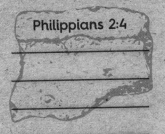

_____

_____

_____

Hebrews 13:16

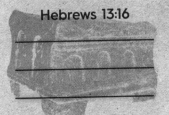

_____

_____

_____

1 Thessalonians 5:14

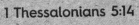

_____

_____

_____

_____

Colossians 3:12

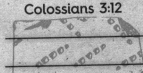

_____

_____

_____

_____

Romans 12:14

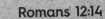

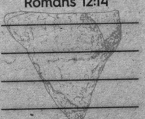

_____

_____

_____

_____

Mark 9:35

_____

_____

_____

_____

...serve, but to serve, and to give his life as a ransom for Matthew 20:28

MAP OF JERUSALEM

1. Gihon Spring (Ancient pottery shards found with Hebrew inscription believed to be related to 2 Chronicles 20:14.)

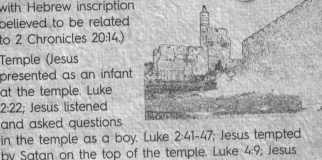

2. Temple (Jesus presented as an infant at the temple. Luke 2:22; Jesus listened and asked questions in the temple as a boy. Luke 2:41-47; Jesus tempted by Satan on the top of the temple. Luke 4:9; Jesus cleansed the temple. John 2:13-16; Jesus taught at the temple during the Feast of Dedication. John 10:22-42)

3. Pool of Siloam (Blind man washed mud from his eyes and was healed. John 9:7)

4. Pool of Bethesda (Jesus healed the paralytic. John 5:2-9)

5. Mount of Olives (Jesus told two of His disciples to get the colt He would ride into Jerusalem. Mark 11:1-2)

6. Garden of Gethsemane (Jesus prayed in the garden before His arrest and death. Matthew 26:36)

7. Caiaphas' House (Steps Jesus' walked after He was arrested. John 18:28)

8. Golgotha (Approximate site of the crucifixion. John 19:17)

9. Approximate location of the Tomb of Jesus (Joseph of Arimathea's tomb where Jesus was buried. Matthew 27:58-60)

10. Approximate location of the Upper Room (Jesus appeared to 10 apostles. John 20:19-21; Jesus to all the disciples. John 20:26-29)

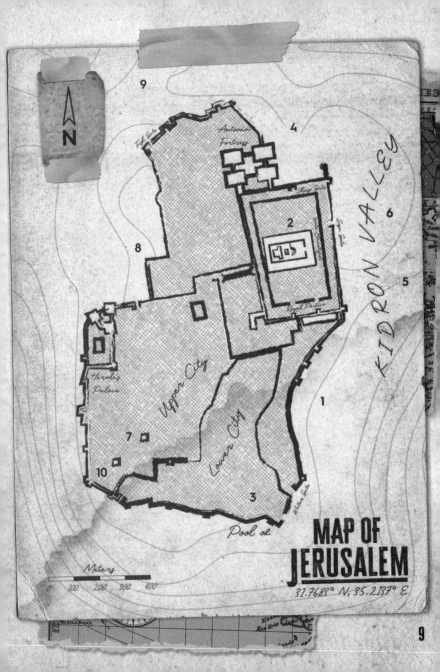

N

KIDRON VALLEY

9

4

Antonia Fortress

6

2

8

5

Herod's Palace

Upper City

Lower City

1

7

10

3

Pool of

MAP OF JERUSALEM

31.7683° N, 35.2137° E

Meters

0   100   200   300   400

DAY 4—TRUTH: JESUS DIED AND ROSE AGAIN

few round tomb stone

Jesus Is Alive (Isaiah 53:5,9–11; John 19:17–20:18)

God told prophets that Jesus would be born and that He would die for our sins. God also said that Jesus would die with the wicked, be buried with the rich, and be raised from the dead. Just as God said, Jesus was crucified between two criminals and Joseph of Arimathea, a wealthy man, buried Jesus' body in Joseph's tomb. A stone was rolled in front of the tomb. On the first day of the week, Mary Magdalene went to the tomb. The stone had been rolled away, and Jesus was gone. Peter and John came to the tomb and saw the burial clothes, but Jesus was not there. While Mary stood outside the tomb crying, a man she thought was a gardener appeared. The Man called her name and immediately Mary knew He was Jesus. She couldn't wait to tell the disciples that Jesus is alive!

he identity of those burie
rchaeol

VBX 2021

Bonus Verse
John 11:25

Today's Point
Jesus fulfilled God's plan to be our Savior.

DIG SITE

GOSPEL VERSES

Use the code in the bottom corner to decode the missing words and learn more about the gospel!

1. All have turned away; all alike have become |03|15|18|18|21|16|20|. There is no one who does good, not even one. Psalm 53:3

2. But God, who is rich in |13|05|18|03|25|, because of his great love that he had for us, made us alive with Christ even though we were dead in trespasses. You are saved by |07|18|01|03|05|! Ephesians 2:4-5

3. Christ |18|05|04|05|05|13|05|04| us from the curse of the |12|01|23| by becoming a curse for us, because it is written, "Cursed is everyone who is hung on a tree". Galatians 3:13

4. For God was pleased to have all his fullness dwell in him, and through him to |18|05|03|15|14|03|09|12|05| everything to himself, whether things on earth or things in heaven, by making peace through his blood, shed on the |03|18|15|19|19|. Colossians 1:19-20

5. For I passed on to you as most important what I also received: that |03|08|18|09|19|20| died for our |19|09|14|19| according to the Scriptures, that he was buried, that he was raised on the |20|08|09|18|04| day according to the Scriptures. 1 Corinthians 15:3-4

few round tomb stones have

Philip Told the Good News
(Isaiah 53:7-8; Acts 8:26-40)

While Philip was preaching in Samaria, an angel of the Lord told him to go south to the road that goes to Gaza. Philip obeyed the angel. Philip saw a man traveling in a chariot. The man was reading a copy of the Isaiah scroll. Philip asked the man if he understood what he was reading. The man said he did not and that he needed someone to explain it to him. Philip explained the good news about Jesus to the man. The man believed what Philip told him and believed in Jesus. Philip baptized the man, and the man went on his way rejoicing.

Bonus Verse
Romans 1:16

Today's Point
The Bible is true and helps us tell others about Jesus.

because it is the power of God for salvation to ev... first to the ... Greek

CATALOG THE VERSE

The Bible is God's story. From beginning to end, God's Word gives us insight into His plan for His creation. And He invites us to become a part of His story. The four major themes of God's story include: Creation (God made the world and everything in it and it was good); Fall (man's choice to rebel against God's good commands which brought sin and death into the world); Redemption (God's plan to redeem His broken creation through Jesus' death and resurrection); Restoration (God will make all things new and sin/death will be no more).

Creation   *Fall*   *Redemption*   *Restoration*

_____   _____   _____   _____

_____   _____   _____   _____

_____   _____   _____   _____

Catalog Bible verses under one of the images representing the major themes of the Bible.

Genesis 1-2   Joel 2:25-26
Romans 5:12   Hebrews 9:15
Galatians 2:20   Ephesians 1:7
Romans 3:23   2 Corinthians 5:17
Acts 17:28   Revelation 21:1-5
Genesis 3:1-7   Isaiah 40:28

10 TRUTHS ABOUT JESUS

1. Jesus is God—John 1:1,14; John 20:28
2. Jesus is the image of the invisible God—Colossians 1:15
3. Jesus is Truth—John 14:6
4. Jesus is the only mediator between God and man—1 Timothy 2:5
5. Jesus forgives and cleanses us from our sin—1 John 1:9
6. Jesus brings us ultimate joy—John 15:11
7. Jesus offers us eternal life—John 10:28
8. Jesus is faithful and will be with us always—Matthew 28:20
9. Jesus gives us wisdom and knowledge—Colossians 2:2-3
10. Jesus is making all things new—Revelation 21:5

QUESTIONS TO CONSIDER:

1. How do these truths give you greater love for God?
2. How can you apply these truths to your own life? (Example: Because Jesus is making all things new, I can focus on eternity and not this world.)
3. How can you share these truths with others?

BIBLICAL ARTIFACT SITE MAP

Mark on the map where each artifact was found.

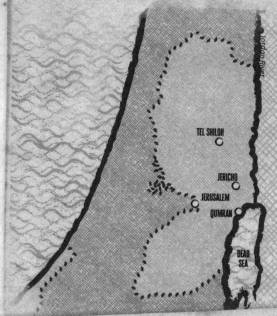

1. **Jericho Ruins**—the ruins provided answers to Jericho's destruction as depicted in the Bible.

2. **Dead Sea Scrolls**—discovered in caves in Qumran and contain biblical fragments of the Old Testament.

3. **Royal Seal of Hezekiah**—discovered at the Ophel, an area between the City of David and the Temple Mount. It is a bulla (a lump of clay holding the impression of a seal that was used to seal documents shut) that read "Belonging to Hezekiah."

4. **Ministers' Bullae**—Bullae of two royal ministers mentioned in Jeremiah 38:1-13. Found at the City of David in Ancient Jerusalem.

5. **Biblical Artifacts at Shiloh**—the site where Joshua divided the Promised Land between the 12 tribes of Israel and where the Tabernacle of the Lord rested for more than 300 years. Artifacts found include pottery, jars, coins, and ceramic pomegranates.

UNCOVER MORE TRUTHS IN THE BIBLE

God's Word helps us to know what is true as it points us to the Truth—Jesus. Making Bible study a daily habit helps us to grow to know Jesus better and apply truth to our lives. We can love God and worship Him through reading His Word. Here are a few simple ways to start reading your Bible in order to uncover the truths found in Scripture:

1. Read the Scripture for what it says. What does the text say? What is the obvious and plain meaning of the text?

2. Know the context of the verse. Be careful not to read a verse in isolation (by itself). Rather, read a few verses before and after the verses to better understand the whole point.

3. Let Scripture interpret Scripture. Go to other passages in the Bible that have a similar word or phrase to better understand the intended meaning. God's Word never contradicts itself.

4. Look for Jesus in the text. All of Scripture points to Jesus. How does the verse reveal who Jesus is or what Jesus has done? How does this verse point you to Jesus?

5. Invite the Holy Spirit to help you understand what the Bible says. God delights for us to know His Word and will help us to understand by the power of the Holy Spirit.

Looking for a place to start reading God's Word? The first four books of the New Testament (the Gospels) are a great place to begin. Choose a book and set a plan to make the reading of God's Word a daily habit.